Happy Hats for Kids

Designs by Kristi Simpson

Designer Kristi Simpson should know what makes kids happy. Not only is she a successful designer, she's also a busy mom of five children! This collection of 15 hats includes designs just right for girls and boys while keeping their little noggins stylishly warm. The little ones in your life may decide they need more than one!

Table of Contents

Hoot Owl
page

Lacy

Skill Level

■■■□ INTERMEDIATE

Finished Sizes

Instructions given fit child's size small; changes for medium and large are in [ ].

Finished Measurements

Circumference: 20 (small) [24 (medium), 24 (large)] inches

Height: 7½ (small) [7½ (medium), 8 (large)] inches

Materials

- Premier Yarns Home Cotton medium (worsted) weight cotton/polyester yarn (2¾ oz/140 yds/80g per skein):
  1 skein each #3813 pastel blue, #3802 cream and #3806 orange
- Sizes F/5/3.75 and H/8/5mm crochet hook or size needed to obtain gauge
- Tapestry needle

Gauge

Rnds 1–3 = 3¾ inches

Pattern Notes

Join with slip stitch as indicated unless otherwise stated.

Chain-4 at beginning of round counts as first double crochet and chain-1 space unless otherwise stated.

Chain-3 at beginning of round does not count as a stitch unless otherwise stated.

Chain-2 at beginning of round counts as first double crochet unless otherwise stated.

Hat

Rnd 1: With size H hook and blue, ch 5 (sk chs count as first dc and ch-1), [dc, ch 1] 6 [7, 7] times in first ch, **join** (see Pattern Notes) in 4th ch of beg ch-5. (14 [16, 16] sts)

Rnd 2: Ch 4 (see Pattern Notes), (dc, ch 1) in each st around, join in 3rd ch of beg ch-4. (28 [32, 32] sts)

Rnd 3: Ch 3 (see Pattern Notes), dc in first st, (dc, ch 1) in next st, *dc in next st, (dc, ch 1) in next st, rep from * around, join in first dc. (42 [48, 48] sts)

Rnd 4: Ch 3, (dc, ch 1) in first st, (dc, ch 1) in next st, sk next ch-1 sp, *(dc, ch 1) in next st, (dc, ch 1) in next st, sk next ch-1 sp, rep from * around, join in first dc. (56 [64, 64] sts)

Rnd 5: Ch 3 (counts as first dc), dc in first dc, ch 1, sk next ch-1 sp, (dc, ch 1) in next dc, sk next ch-1 sp, *2 dc in next dc, ch 1, sk next ch-1 sp, (dc, ch 1) in next dc, sk next ch-1 sp, rep from * around, join in top of beg ch-3. (70 [80, 80] sts)

Rnd 6: Ch 4, sk next st, *(dc, ch 1) in next st, sk next st, rep from * around, join in 3rd ch of beg ch-4.

Rnd 7: Ch 3, (dc, ch 1) in each ch-1 sp around to last ch-1 sp, dc in last ch-1 sp, join in beg ch-3.

Rnds 8–13 [8–13, 8–15]: [Rep rnds 6 and 7 alternately] 3 [3, 4] times. At end of last rnd, fasten off.

Rnd 14 [14, 16]: With size F hook, join cream in any st, **ch 2** (see Pattern Notes), dc in each st around, join in first dc.

Rnd 15 [15, 17]: Ch 2, *dc in each of next 5 [6, 6] sts, **dc dec** (see Stitch Guide) in next 2 sts, rep from * around, join in first dc. (60 [70, 70] sts)

Rnd 16 [16, 18]: Ch 2, *dc in each of next 4 [5, 5] sts, dc dec in next 2 sts, rep from * around, join in first dc. (50 [60, 60] sts)

Rnd 17 [17, 19]: Ch 2, dc in each st around, join in first dc. Fasten off cream.

Rnd 18 [18, 20]: Join blue in any st, ch 1, sc in each st around, join in beg ch-1. Fasten off blue.

Bow

Row 1: Now working in rows, with size F hook and orange, ch 6, sc in 2nd ch from hook and in each rem ch across, turn. *(5 sc)*

Row 2: Ch 1, working in **back lp** *(see Stitch Guide)*, sc in each st across, turn.

Row 3: Ch 1, working in **front lp** *(see Stitch Guide)*, sc in each st across, turn.

Rows 4–13: [Rep rows 2 and 3 alternately] 5 times. Fasten off.

Wrap strand of orange around center of piece, cinch to form Bow and sew to secure. Sew each end of Bow on Hat using photo as a guide. ●

Bella Bouquet

Skill Level
 INTERMEDIATE

Finished Sizes
Instructions given fit child's size small; changes for medium and large are in [ ].

Finished Measurements
Circumference: 18 *(small)* [20 *(medium)*, 22 *(large)*] inches, before Brim

Height: 7½ *(small)* [8 *(medium)*, 8½ *(large)*] inches

Flower: 2 inches in diameter

Materials
- Bernat Handicrafter Cotton medium (worsted) weight cotton yarn (1¾ oz/80 yds/50g per skein):
  1 skein each #101030 pale yellow, #101111 mod blue, #101699 tangerine, #101740 hot pink and #101712 hot green
- Size H/8/5mm crochet hook or size needed to obtain gauge
- Tapestry needle
- Stitch marker

Gauge
Rnds 1–4 = 2 inches in diameter

Pattern Notes
Weave in ends as work progresses.

Work in continuous rounds; do not turn or join unless otherwise stated.

Mark first stitch of round. Move marker as work progresses.

Join with slip stitch as indicated unless otherwise stated.

Special Stitch
Surface stitch (surface st): Holding yarn at back of work, insert hook between rows, yo, pull lp through st and lp on hook.

Hat
Rnd 1: With yellow, ch 2, 6 sc in first ch, **do not join** *(see Pattern Notes)*, **place marker** *(see Pattern Notes)* in first st. *(6 sts)*

Rnd 2: 2 sc in each st around. *(12 sts)*

Rnd 3: [Sc in next st, 2 sc in next st] around. *(18 sts)*

Rnd 4: [Sc in each of next 2 sts, 2 sc in next st] around. *(24 sts)*

Rnd 5: [Sc in each of next 3 sts, 2 sc in next st] around. *(30 sts)*

Rnd 6: [Sc in each of next 4 sts, 2 sc in next st] around. *(36 sts)*

Rnd 7: [Sc in each of next 5 sts, 2 sc in next st] around. *(42 sts)*

Rnd 8: [Sc in each of next 6 sts, 2 sc in next st] around. *(48 sts)*

Rnd 9: [Sc in each of next 7 sts, 2 sc in next st] around. *(54 sts)*

Rnd 10: [Sc in each of next 8 sts, 2 sc in next st] around. *(60 sts)*

Sizes Medium & Large Only
Rnd [11]: [Sc in each of next 9 sts, 2 sc in next st] around. *([66] sts)*

Size Large Only
Rnd [12]: [Sc in each of next 10 sts, 2 sc in next st] around. *([72] sts)*

All Sizes

Rnds 11–16 [12–18, 13–19]: Sc in each st around. In last st of last rnd, **change color** (see Stitch Guide) to blue. Fasten off yellow. (60 [66, 72] sts)

Rnds 17–28 [19–34, 20–40]: Sc in each st around.

Brim

Size Small Only

Rnd 29: [Sc in each of next 9 sts, 2 sc in next st] around. (66 sts)

Sizes Small & Medium Only

Rnd 30 [35]: [Sc in each of next 10 sts, 2 sc in next st] around. (72 sts)

All Sizes

Rnd 31 [36, 41]: [Sc in each of next 11 sts, 2 sc in next st] around. (78 sts)

Rnd 32 [37, 42]: [Sc in each of next 12 sts, 2 sc in next st] around. (84 sts)

Sizes Medium & Large Only

Rnd [38, 43]: [Sc in each of next 13 sts, 2 sc in next st] around. ([90] sts)

Size Large Only

Rnd [44]: [Sc in each of next 14 sts, 2 sc in next st] around. ([96] sts)

All Sizes

Rnd 33 [39, 45]: Sc in each st around, **join** (see Pattern Notes) in first st. Fasten off.

Trim

Weave a strand of yellow through sts of last rnd of Hat.

Flower

Make 2 pink, 1 tangerine, 1 yellow & 1 blue.

Row 1: Ch 30, sc in 2nd ch from hook and in each of next 5 chs, hdc in each of next 10 chs, dc in each rem ch across. Leaving long tail for sewing, fasten off.

Beg with sc at center and sewing as work progresses, spiral foundation ch to form Flower. Using photo as a guide, position Flower on Hat at color change and sew in place.

Stem
Make 5.

Join green with sl st under center of Flower, **surface st** (see Special Stitch) down Hat to Brim using photo as a guide. Rep for each Flower, making sure to cross each Stem at same middle point. Insert strand of yellow from front to back to front around center cross point of Stems and tie in a bow to secure. ●

Hoot Owl

Skill Level

 **EASY**

Finished Sizes

Instructions given fit child's size small; changes for medium and large are in [ ].

Finished Measurements

Circumference: 18 *(small)* [20 *(medium)*, 22 *(large)*] inches, above Earflaps

Height: 7 *(small)* [7½ *(medium)*, 8 *(large)*] inches, excluding Earflaps and Ears

---

Materials

- Premier Yarns Deborah Norville Everyday Soft Worsted medium (worsted) weight acrylic yarn (4 oz/203 yds/113g per skein):
  - 1 skein each #1011 chocolate, #1028 mustard, #1015 sagebrush and #1002 cream
- Size H/8/5mm crochet hook or size needed to obtain gauge
- Tapestry needle
- Stitch marker

Gauge

Rnds 1–7 = 3 inches in diameter

Pattern Notes

Weave in ends as work progresses. Move marker as work progresses.

Hat is worked in continuous rounds; do not turn or join unless otherwise stated.

Mark first stitch of round. Move marker as work progresses.

Join with slip stitch as indicated unless otherwise stated.

To change color, finish last stitch, drop old color, yarn over with new color and pull through st to join round.

Hat

Rnd 1: With chocolate, ch 2, 6 sc in first ch, **do not join** *(see Pattern Notes)*, **place marker** *(see Pattern Notes)* in first st. *(6 sts)*

Rnd 2: 2 sc in each st around. *(12 sts)*

Rnd 3: [Sc in next st, 2 sc in next st] around. *(18 sts)*

Rnd 4: [Sc in each of next 2 sts, 2 sc in next st] around. *(24 sts)*

Rnd 5: [Sc in each of next 3 sts, 2 sc in next st] around. *(30 sts)*

Rnd 6: [Sc in each of next 4 sts, 2 sc in next st] around. *(36 sts)*

Rnd 7: [Sc in each of next 5 sts, 2 sc in next st] around. *(42 sts)*

Rnd 8: [Sc in each of next 6 sts, 2 sc in next st] around. *(48 sts)*

Rnd 9: [Sc in each of next 7 sts, 2 sc in next st] around. *(54 sts)*

Rnd 10: [Sc in each of next 8 sts, 2 sc in next st] around. *(60 sts)*

Sizes Medium & Large Only

Rnd [11]: [Sc in each of next 9 sts, 2 sc in next st] around. *([66] sts)*

Size Large Only

Rnd [12]: [Sc in each of next 10 sts, 2 sc in next st] around. *([72] sts)*

All Sizes

Rnds 11–29 [12–34, 13–41]: Sc in each st around.

Rnd 30 [35, 42]: Sc in each st around, join in first st. Fasten off.

Earflap

Getting started: Fold Hat in half and mark st on each side of last rnd.

Row 1: Now working in rows, **join** *(see Pattern Notes)* chocolate in first marked st, ch 1, sc in same st and in each of next 8 sts, leaving rem sts unworked, turn. *(9 sc)*

Rows 2–6: Ch 1, sc in each st across, turn.

Row 7: Ch 1, **sc dec** *(see Stitch Guide)* in first 2 sts, sc in each of next 5 sts, sc dec in last 2 sts, turn. *(7 sts)*

Row 8: Ch 1, sc dec in first 2 sts, sc in each of next 3 sts, sc dec in last 2 sts, turn. *(5 sts)*

Row 9: Ch 1, sc dec in first 2 sts, sc in next st, sc dec in last 2 sts. Fasten off. *(3 sts)*

Rep at marker on opposite side of Hat for 2nd Earflap.

Edging

Rnd 1: Now working in rnds, holding 1 strand each mustard and sagebrush tog, join in first st at back of Hat, ch 1, sc in each st around Hat, working 1 sc in each row end along sides of Earflaps, join in first st. Fasten off.

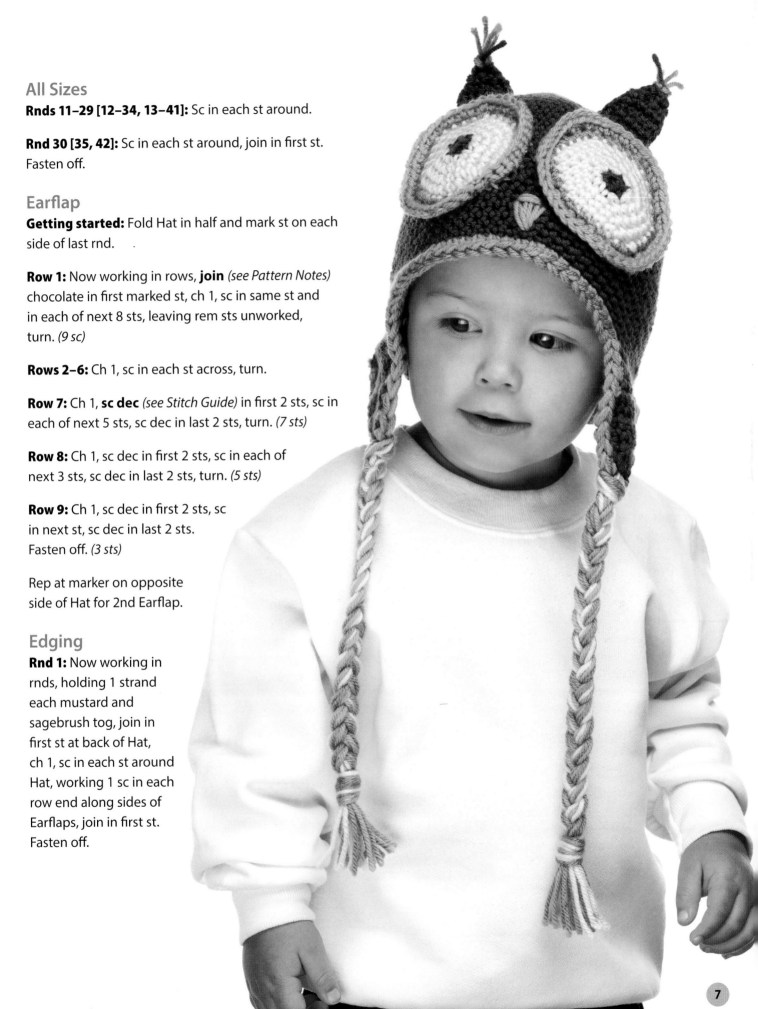

Eye
Make 2.

Rnd 1: With chocolate, ch 2, 6 sc in first ch, **change color** (see Pattern Notes) to cream, join in first sc. Fasten off chocolate. *(6 sc)*

Rnd 2: Ch 1, 2 sc in each sc around, join in first sc. *(12 sc)*

Rnd 3: Ch 1, [sc in next sc, 2 sc in next sc] around, join in first sc. *(18 sc)*

Rnd 4: Ch 1, [sc in each of next 2 sc, 2 sc in next sc] around, join in first sc. *(24 sc)*

Rnd 5: Ch 1, [sc in each of next 3 sc, 2 sc in next sc] around, change color to sagebrush, join in first sc. Fasten off cream. *(30 sc)*

Rnd 6: Ch 1, [sc in each of next 4 sc, 2 sc in next sc] around, change color to mustard, join in first sc. Fasten off sagebrush. *(36 sc)*

Rnd 7: Ch 1, [sc in each of next 5 sc, 2 sc in next sc] around, join in first sc. Leaving long tail for sewing, fasten off. *(42 sc)*

Working around posts of sts on last rnd, sew Eye to Hat using photo as a guide.

Nose
With mustard, using **satin stitch** (see illustration), embroider Nose on Hat between Eyes as shown in photo.

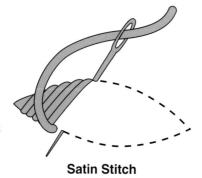

Satin Stitch

Ear
Make 2.

Row 1: With chocolate, ch 6, sc in 2nd ch from hook and in each rem ch across, turn. *(5 sc)*

Rows 2–4: Ch 1, sc in each st across, turn.

Row 5: Ch 1, **sc dec** (see Stitch Guide) in first 2 sc, sc in next sc, sc dec in last 2 sc, turn. *(3 sts)*

Row 6: Ch 1, sc dec in first 2 sts, sc dec in 2nd and 3rd st, turn. *(2 sts)*

Row 7: Ch 1, sc dec in first 2 sts. Fasten off.

Sew Ear on top of Hat 5 rnds from center as shown in photo. Cut 1 strand each chocolate, mustard and sagebrush. Holding strands tog, fold strands in half, pull fold through st on last row, pull ends through fold. Pull to tighten.

Tie
Make 2.

Cut 2 strands each mustard, sagebrush and cream, each 3 feet in length. Holding strands tog, fold strands in half, pull fold through center st at bottom of Earflap, pull ends through fold. Pull to tighten. Braid strands and secure end of braid with a knot. Trim as desired. ●

Stripes & Pom

Skill Level
 INTERMEDIATE

Finished Sizes
Instructions given fit child's size small; changes for medium and large are in [ ].

Finished Measurements
Circumference: 17 *(small)* [22 *(medium)*, 25 *(large)*] inches

Height: 8¼ *(small)* [9 *(medium)*, 9¼ *(large)*] inches, excluding Pompom and Earflaps

Materials
- Cascade Yarns Cherub Aran medium (worsted) weight nylon/acrylic yarn (3½ oz/240 yds/100g per skein):
  - 1 skein each #28 boy blue, #09 ecru and #11 key lime
- Size G/6/4mm crochet hook or size needed to obtain gauge
- Tapestry needle
- Stitch marker
- 6-inch wide piece of cardboard

Gauge
Ribbing: 8 sts = 2 inches; 7 rows = 2 inches

Body: 8 sts = 2 inches; 10 rnds = 2½ inches

Pattern Notes
Weave in ends as work progresses.

Ribbing section is worked first from side to side, increasing and decreasing to create Earflaps, then stitches for body of Hat are worked in side of Ribbing rows.

Ribbing is worked in back loops unless otherwise stated.

Join with slip stitch as indicated unless otherwise stated.

To change color, finish last stitch, drop old color, pick up new color and continue with next round.

Hat

Ribbing
Row 1: With blue, ch 9, sc in 2nd ch from hook and in each rem ch across, turn. *(8 sc)*

Row 2: Ch 1, working in **back lp** *(see Stitch Guide and Pattern Notes)*, sc in each st across, turn.

Rows 3–7: Rep row 2.

Sizes Medium & Large Only
Rows [8–10]: Rep row 2.

Size Large Only
Rows [11–13]: Rep row 2.

All Sizes

First Earflap
Row 8 [11, 14]: Ch 1, 2 sc in first st, sc in each rem st, turn. *(9 sc)*

Row 9 [12, 15]: Ch 1, sc in each st across to last st, 2 sc in last st. *(10 sts)*

Rows 10 & 11 [13 & 14, 16 & 17]: Rep rows 8 and 9 [11 and 12, 14 and 15]. *(12 sts)*

Row 12 [15, 18]: Rep row 8 [11, 14]. *(13 sts)*

Rows 13–15 [16–18, 19–21]: Rep row 2.

Row 20 [23, 26]: Rep row 16 [19, 22]. *(8 sts)*

Rows 21–36 [24–47, 27–54]: Rep row 2.

2nd Earflap

Row 37 [48, 55]: Rep row 9 [12, 15]. *(9 sts)*

Rows 38–41 [49–52, 56–59]: [Rep rows 8 & 9 [11 & 12, 14 & 15] alternately] twice. *(13 sts)*

Rows 42–44 [53–55, 60–62]: Rep row 2.

Row 45 [56, 63]: Rep row 17 [20, 23]. *(12 sts)*

Rows 46–49 [57–60, 64–67]: [Rep rows 16 & 17 [19 & 20, 22 & 23] alternately] twice. *(8 sts)*

Rows 50–60 [61–76, 68–88]: Rep row 2.

Leaving long end for sewing, fasten off.

With long end and working in back lp of last row and front lp of first row, sew Ribbing tog.

Body

Rnd 1: Now working in rnds and working in ends of Ribbing rows on even side, **join** *(see Pattern Notes)* ecru in first st at seam, ch 1, sc in each row end around, join in first st. *(60 [76, 88] sts)*

Rnd 2: Ch 1, **bpsc** *(see Stitch Guide)* in each st around, join in beg ch-1, **drop ecru** *(see Pattern Notes)*.

Rnd 3: Join lime in first st, ch 1, sc in each st around, join in beg ch-1.

Rnd 4: Ch 1, bpsc around each st around, join in beg ch-1, drop lime.

Rnd 5: Join blue in first st, ch 1, sc in each st around, join in beg ch-1.

Rnd 6: Ch 1, bpsc around each st around, join in beg ch-1, drop blue.

Rnd 7: With ecru, ch 1, sc in each st around, join in beg ch-1.

Row 16 [19, 22]: Ch 1, sc in first st, **sc dec** *(see Stitch Guide)* in next 2 sts, sc in each rem st across, turn. *(12 sts)*

Row 17 [20, 23]: Ch 1, sc in each st across to last 3 sts, sc dec in next 2 sts, sc in last st, turn. *(11 sts)*

Rows 18 & 19 [21 & 22, 24 & 25]: Rep rows 16 and 17 [19 and 20, 22 and 23]. *(9 sts)*

Rnd 8: Ch 1, bpsc around each st around, join in beg ch-1, drop ecru.

Rnds 9 & 10: With lime, rep rnds 3 and 4.

Rnds 11 & 12: With blue, rep rnds 5 and 6.

Rnds 13 & 14: With ecru, rep rnds 7 and 8. At end of last rnd, fasten off ecru.

Rnds 15 & 16: With lime, rep rnds 3 and 4. At end of last rnd, fasten off lime.

Size Small Only

Rnd 17: With blue, ch 1, sc in each of first 8 sts, sc dec in next 2 sts, *sc in each of next 8 sts, sc dec in next 2 sts, rep from * around, join in beg ch-1. *(54 sts)*

Size Medium Only

Rnd [17]: With blue, ch 1, sc in each of first 17 sts, sc dec in next 2 sts, *sc in each of next 17 sts, sc dec in next 2 sts, rep from * around, join in beg ch-1. *([72] sts)*

Rnd [18]: Ch 1, sc in each of first 10 sts, sc dec in next 2 sts, *sc in each of next 10 sts, sc dec in next 2 sts, rep from * around, join in beg ch-1. *([66] sts)*

Size Large Only

Rnds [17 & 18]: With blue, ch 1, sc in each st around, join in beg ch-1.

Sizes Medium & Large Only

Rnd [19]: Ch 1, sc in each of first 9 sts, sc dec in next 2 sts, *sc in each of next 9 sts, sc dec in next 2 sts, rep from * around, join in beg ch-1. *([60, 80] sts)*

Rnd [20]: Ch 1, sc in each of first 8 sts, sc dec in next 2 sts, *sc in each of next 8 sts, sc dec in next 2 sts, rep from * around, join in beg ch-1. *([54, 72] sts)*

All Sizes

Rnd 18 [21, 21]: Ch 1, sc in each of first 7 sts, sc dec in next 2 sts, *sc in each of next 7 sts, sc dec in next 2 sts, rep from * around, join in beg ch-1. *(48 [48, 64] sts)*

Rnd 19 [22, 22]: Ch 1, sc in each of first 6 sts, sc dec in next 2 sts, *sc in each of next 6 sts, sc dec in next 2 sts, rep from * around, join in beg ch-1. *(42 [42, 56] sts)*

Rnd 20 [23, 23]: Ch 1, sc in each of first 5 sts, sc dec in next 2 sts, *sc in each of next 5 sts, sc dec in next 2 sts, rep from * around, join in beg ch-1. *(36 [36, 48] sts)*

Rnd 21 [24, 24]: Ch 1, sc in each of first 4 sts, sc dec in next 2 sts, *sc in each of next 4 sts, sc dec in next 2 sts, rep from * around, join in beg ch-1. *(30 [30, 40] sts)*

Rnd 22 [25, 25]: Ch 1, sc in each of first 3 sts, sc dec in next 2 sts, *sc in each of next 3 sts, sc dec in next 2 sts, rep from * around, join in beg ch-1. *(24 [24, 32] sts)*

Rnd 23 [26, 26]: Ch 1, sc in each of first 2 sts, sc dec in next 2 sts, *sc in each of next 2 sts, sc dec in next 2 sts, rep from * around, join in beg ch-1. *(18 [18, 24] sts)*

Size Large Only

Rnd [27]: Ch 1, sc in first st, sc dec in next 2 sts, *sc in next st, sc dec in next 2 sts, rep from * around, join in beg ch-1. *([16] sts)*

All Sizes

Rnd 24 [27, 28]: Ch 1, [sc dec in next 2 sts] 9 [9, 8] times, join in beg ch-1. *(9 [9, 8] sts)*

Rnd 25 [28, 29]: Ch 1, sc in each st around, join in beg ch-1. Leaving long end, fasten off.

Weave end through sts of last rnd and pull to close.

Pompom
Make 1.

Wrap strand of blue around cardboard 40 times or to desired thickness. Remove from cardboard and tie in center with 4-inch strand of same color. Cut lps and trim ends to desired shape. Use center strand to tie Pompom securely to top of Hat. ●

Sweet & Sassy

Skill Level
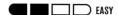 EASY

Finished Sizes
Instructions given fit child's size small; changes for medium and large are in [ ].

Finished Measurements
Circumference: 18 (small) [20 (medium), 22 (large)] inches, excluding Brim

Height: 3½ (small) [3½ (medium), 4 (large)] inches

Materials
- Plymouth Yarn Encore Worsted medium (worsted) weight acrylic/wool yarn (3½ oz/200 yds/100g per skein):
    1 skein each #0456 harvest, #0462 woodbine and #0517 denim blue
- Size H/8/5mm crochet hook or size needed to obtain gauge
- Tapestry needle
- Stitch marker
- Sewing needle and matching thread
- ¾-inch brown button: 4

Gauge
Rnds 1–4 = 2 inches in diameter

Pattern Notes
Weave in ends as work progresses. Move marker as work progresses.

Work in continuous rounds; do not turn or join unless otherwise stated.

Mark first stitch of round. Move marker as work progressses.

Join with slip stitch as indicated unless otherwise stated.

Hat
Rnd 1: With harvest, ch 2, 6 sc in first ch, **do not join** (see Pattern Notes), **place marker** (see Pattern Notes) in first st. (6 sts)

Rnd 2: 2 sc in each st around. (12 sts)

Rnd 3: [Sc in next st, 2 sc in next st] around. (18 sts)

Rnd 4: [Sc in each of next 2 sts, 2 sc in next st] around. (24 sts)

Rnd 5: [Sc in each of next 3 sts, 2 sc in next st] around. (30 sts)

Rnd 6: [Sc in each of next 4 sts, 2 sc in next st] around. (36 sts)

Rnd 7: [Sc in each of next 5 sts, 2 sc in next st] around. (42 sts)

Rnd 8: [Sc in each of next 6 sts, 2 sc in next st] around. (48 sts)

Rnd 9: [Sc in each of next 7 sts, 2 sc in next st] around. (54 sts)

Rnd 10: [Sc in each of next 8 sts, 2 sc in next st] around. (60 sts)

Rnd 11: [Sc in each of next 9 sts, 2 sc in next st] around. (66 sts)

Rnd 12: [Sc in each of next 10 sts, 2 sc in next st] around. (72 sts)

Rnd 13: [Sc in each of next 11 sts, 2 sc in next st] around. (78 sts)

Sizes Medium & Large Only

Rnd [14]: [Sc in each of next 12 sts, 2 sc in next st] around. ([84] sts)

Size Large Only

Rnd [15]: [Sc in each of next 13 sts, 2 sc in next st] around. ([90] sts)

All Sizes

Rnd 14 [15, 16]: Working in **back lp** (see Stitch Guide), sc in each st around. (78 [84, 90] sts)

Rnd 15 [16, 17]: Working in both lps, sc in each st around.

Size Large Only

Rnd [18]: [Sc in each of next 13 sts, **sc dec** (see Stitch Guide) in next 2 sts] around. ([84] sts)

Sizes Medium & Large Only

Rnd [17, 19]: [Sc in each of next 12 sts, sc dec in next 2 sts] around. ([78] sts)

All Sizes

Rnd 16 [18, 20]: [Sc in each of next 11 sts, sc dec in next 2 sts] around. (72 sts)

Sizes Small & Medium Only

Rnd 17 [19]: [Sc in each of next 10 sts, sc dec in next 2 sts] around. (66 sts)

Size Small Only

Rnd 18: [Sc in each of next 9 sts, sc dec in next 2 sts] around. (60 sts)

All Sizes

Rnds 19–29 [20–30, 21–33]: Sc in each st around. (60 [66, 72] sts)

Rnd 30 [31, 34]: Turn, working in back lp, sc in each st around.

Brim

Rnds 31–33 [32–34, 35–38]: Sc in each st around.

Rnd 34 [35, 39]: Sc in each st around, **join** (see Pattern Notes) in first st. Fasten off.

Flower

Make 2 each in woodbine & blue.

Rnd 1: Ch 4, sl st in first ch to form ring, ch 1, 5 sc in ring, do not join. (5 sc)

Rnd 2: (Sl st, ch 1, 2 dc, ch 1, sl st) in each st around, join in first st. Fasten off. (5 petals)

Finishing

Fold up Brim. Sew buttons on Hat as shown in photo. Push button through center of Flower. ●

Mosaic

Skill Level
■■■□ INTERMEDIATE

Finished Sizes
Instructions given fit child's size small; changes for medium and large are in [ ].

Finished Measurements
Circumference: 19 (small) [19 (medium), 20¾ (large)] inches

Height: 7½ (small) [8 (medium), 8½ (large)] inches

Materials

- Premier Yarns Deborah Norville Everyday Soft Worsted medium (worsted) weight acrylic yarn (4 oz/203 yds/113g per skein):
    1 skein each #1002 cream and #1021 magenta
- Size H/8/5mm crochet hook or size needed to obtain gauge
- Tapestry needle

Gauge
Rnds 1–3 = 3¼ inches in diameter

Pattern Notes
Weave in ends as work progresses.

Join with slip stitch as indicated unless otherwise stated.

Chain-2 at beginning of round does not count as a stitch unless otherwise stated.

To change color, finish last stitch, drop old color, pick up new color and continue with next round.

Special Stitch
V-stitch (V-st): (Dc, ch 1, dc) in st or sp as indicated.

Hat
Rnd 1: With cream, ch 4, 10 dc in first ch, **join** (see Pattern Notes) in first st. (10 sts)

Rnd 2: Ch 2 (see Pattern Notes), 2 dc in each st around, join in first st. (20 sts)

Rnd 3: Ch 2, dc in first st, 2 dc in next st, *dc in next st, 2 dc in next st, rep from * around, join in first st. (30 sts)

Rnd 4: Ch 2, dc in each of first 2 sts, 2 dc in next st, *dc in each of next 2 sts, 2 dc in next st, rep from * around, join in first st. (40 sts)

Rnd 5: Ch 2, dc in each of first 3 sts, 2 dc in next st, *dc in each of next 3 sts, 2 dc in next st, rep from * around, join in first st. (50 sts)

Rnd 6: Ch 2, dc in each of first 4 sts, 2 dc in next st, *dc in each of next 4 sts, 2 dc in next st, rep from * around, join in first st. (60 sts)

Sizes Small & Medium Only
Rnd 7: Ch 2, **V-st** (see Special Stitch) in first st, sk next 2 sts, *V-st in next st, sk next 2 sts, rep from * around, join in first st, **drop cream** (see Pattern Notes). (20 V-sts)

Size Large Only
Rnd [7]: Ch 2, dc in each of first 5 sts, 2 dc in next st, *dc in each of next 5 sts, 2 dc in next st, rep from * around, join in first st. ([70] sts)

Rnd [8]: Ch 2, V-st in first st, sk next 2 sts, *V-st in next st, sk next 2 sts, rep from * around to last 4 sts, V-st in next st, sk last 3 sts, join in first st, drop cream. (23 V-sts)

All Sizes

Rnd 8 [8, 9]: Join magenta in first st, ch 2, 3 dc in ch-1 sp of each V-st around, join in first st, drop magenta. *(60 [60, 69] dc)*

Rnd 9 [9, 10]: With cream, ch 2, V-st in sp between each V-st 2 rnds below around, join in first st, drop cream.

Rnds 10–15 [10–17, 11–18]: [Rep rnds 8 and 9 [8 and 9, 9 and 10] alternately] 3 [4, 4] times. At end of last rnd, fasten off magenta.

Rnd 16 [18, 19]: Ch 2, dc in each st and ch sp around, join in first st. *(60 [60, 69] sts)*

Sizes Small & Medium Only

Rnd 17 [19]: Ch 2, dc in each of first 8 sts, **dc dec** *(see Stitch Guide)* in next 2 sts, *dc in each of next 8 sts, dc dec in next 2 sts, rep from * around, join in first st. *(54 sts)*

Fasten off cream.

Size Large Only

Rnd [20]: Ch 2, dc in each of first 7 sts, **dc dec** *(see Stitch Guide)* in next 2 sts, *dc in each of next 7 sts, dc dec in next 2 sts, rep from * around, join in first st. *([62] sts)*

Fasten off cream.

All Sizes

Rnd 18 [20, 21]: Join magenta in first st, ch 1, sc in each st around, join in first st. Fasten off magenta. ●

Classic

Skill Level
 **EASY**

Finished Sizes
Instructions given fit child's size small; changes for medium and large are in [ ].

Finished Measurements
Circumference: 18 (small) [20 (medium), 21 (large)] inches

Height: 6½ (small) [7¾ (medium), 8½ (large)] inches

Materials

- Ewe Ewe Yarns Wooly Worsted medium (worsted) weight superwash merino yarn (1¾ oz/ 95 yds/50g per skein):
    1 skein each #90 vanilla, #75 sky blue and #92 wheat
- Size F/5/3.75mm crochet hook or size needed to obtain gauge
- Tapestry needle
- Stitch marker

Gauge
Rnds 1–3 = 2½ inches in diameter

Pattern Notes
Weave in ends as work progresses.

When changing color, do not fasten off old color unless otherwise stated.

Join with slip stitch as indicated unless otherwise stated.

Work in joined rounds with right side always facing; do not turn unless otherwise stated.

Mark first stitch of round. Move marker as work progresses.

Chain-2 at beginning of round does not count as stitch unless otherwise stated.

Hat
Rnd 1 (RS): With vanilla, ch 2, 10 [10, 12] dc in first ch, **changing color** (see Stitch Guide and Pattern Notes) to blue in last st, **join** (see Pattern Notes) in first st, **place marker** (see Pattern Notes) in first st. (10 [10, 12] sts)

Rnd 2: Ch 1, 2 sc in each st around, changing color to vanilla in last st, join in first st. (20 [20, 24] sts)

Rnd 3: Ch 2 (see Pattern Notes), dc in first st, 2 dc in next st, *dc in next st, 2 dc in next st, rep from * around, changing color to wheat in last st, join in first st. (30 [30, 36] sts)

Rnd 4: Ch 1, sc in each of first 2 sts, 2 sc in next st, *sc in each of next 2 sts, 2 sc in next st, rep from * around, changing color to vanilla in last st, join in first st. (40 [40, 48] sts)

Rnd 5: Ch 2, dc in each of first 3 sts, 2 dc in next st, *dc in each of next 3 sts, 2 dc in next st, rep from * around, changing color to blue in last st, join in first st. (50 [50, 60] sts)

Rnd 6: Ch 1, sc in each of first 4 sts, 2 sc in next st, *sc in each of next 4 sts, 2 sc in next st, rep from * around, changing color to vanilla in last st, join in first st. (60 [60, 72] sts)

Rnd 7: Ch 2, dc in each of first 5 sts, 2 dc in next st, *dc in each of next 5 sts, 2 dc in next st, rep from * around, changing color to wheat in last st, join in first st. (70 [70, 84] sts)

Sizes Small & Large Only

Rnd 8: With wheat, ch 1, sc in each st around, changing to vanilla in last st, join in first st.

Size Medium Only

Rnd [8]: With wheat, ch 1, sc in each of first 6 sts, 2 sc in next st, *sc in each of next 6 sts, 2 sc in next st, rep from * around, changing color to vanilla in last st, join in first st. *([80] sts)*

All Sizes

Rnd 9: With vanilla, ch 2, dc in each st around, changing color to blue in last st, join in first st.

Rnd 10: Ch 1, sc in each st around, changing color to vanilla in last st, join in first st.

Rnd 11: Ch 2, dc in each st around, changing color to wheat in last st, join in first st.

Sizes Small & Large Only

Rnds 12–15 [12–19]: [Rep rnds 8–11] 1 [2] time(s). At end of last rnd, fasten off vanilla and blue.

Size Medium Only

Rnd [12]: With wheat, ch 1, sc in each st around, changing color to vanilla in last st, join in first st.

Rnds [13–16]: Rep rnds 9–12.

Rnds [17–19]: Rep rnds 9–11. At end of last rnd, fasten off vanilla and blue.

All Sizes

Rnds 16–20 [20–25, 20–26]: With wheat, ch 2, dc in each st around, join in first st.

Rnd 21 [26, 27]: Turn, ch 2, working in **back lp** *(see Stitch Guide)*, dc in each st around, join in first st.

Rnds 22 & 23 [27 & 28, 28–31]: Ch 2, dc in each st around, join in first st.

Rnd 24 [29, 32]: Ch 2, dc in each st around, changing color to vanilla in last st, join in first st.

Rnd 25 [30, 33]: Ch 1, sc in each st around, changing color to wheat in last st, join in first st.

Rnd 26 [31, 34]: Ch 2, dc in each st around, join in first st. Fasten off. ●

Newsboy

Skill Level
■■□□ EASY

Finished Sizes
Instructions given fit child's size small; changes for medium and large are in [ ].

Finished Measurements
Circumference: 16 (small) [19 (medium), 22 (large)] inches

Height: 7½ (small) [8 (medium), 8½ (large)] inches

Materials
- Plymouth Yarn Encore Dynamo medium (worsted) weight acrylic/wool yarn (3½ oz/200 yds/100g per skein):
  1 skein #0043 stonewashed
- Size F/5/3.75mm crochet hook or size needed to obtain gauge
- Tapestry needle
- Stitch marker

Gauge
Rnds 1–4 = 4 inches in diameter

Pattern Notes
Weave in ends as work progresses.

Work in continuous rounds; do not turn or join unless otherwise stated.

Mark first stitch of round. Move marker as work progresses.

Join with slip stitch as indicated unless otherwise stated.

Hat
Rnd 1: Ch 4, 10 dc in first ch, **do not join** (see Pattern Notes), **place marker** (see Pattern Notes) in first st. (10 sts)

Rnd 2: 2 sc in next st, 2 hdc in next st, 2 dc in each rem st around. (20 sts)

Rnd 3: [Dc in next st, 2 dc in next st] around. (30 sts)

Rnd 4: [Dc in each of next 2 sts, 2 dc in next st] around. (40 sts)

Rnd 5: [Dc in each of next 3 sts, 2 dc in next st] around. (50 sts)

Rnd 6: [Dc in each of next 4 sts, 2 dc in next st] around. (60 sts)

Rnd 7: [Dc in each of next 5 sts, 2 dc in next st] around. (70 sts)

Rnd 8: [Dc in each of next 6 sts, 2 dc in next st] around. (80 sts)

Sizes Medium & Large Only
Rnd [9]: [Dc in each of next 7 sts, 2 dc in next st] around. ([90] sts)

Size Large Only
Rnd [10]: [Dc in each of next 8 sts, 2 dc in next st] around. ([100] sts)

All Sizes
Rnds 9–11 [10–12, 11–13]: Dc in each st around.

Rnd 12 [13, 14]: [Dc in each of next 6 [7, 8] sts, **dc dec** (see Stitch Guide) in next 2 sts] around. (70 [80, 90] sts)

Rnd 13 [14, 15]: [Dc in each of next 5 [6, 7] sts, dc dec in next 2 sts] around. (60 [70, 80] sts)

Rnd 14 [15, 16]: [Dc in each of next 4 [5, 6] sts, dc dec in next 2 sts] around. *(50 [60, 70] sts)*

Rnd 15 [16, 17]: Dc in each st around.

Rnds 16 & 17 [17 & 18, 18 & 19]: Sc in each st around. At end of last rnd, **join** *(see Pattern Notes)* in first st. Do not fasten off.

Visor

Row 1: Turn, now working in rows, ch 1, sc in each of next 25 sts, leaving rem sts unworked, turn. *(25 sc)*

Row 2: Ch 1, **sc dec** *(see Stitch Guide)* in first 2 sts, sc in each of next 21 sts, sc dec in last 2 sts, turn. *(23 sts)*

Row 3: Ch 1, sc dec in first 2 sts, sc in each of next 19 sts, sc dec in last 2 sts, turn. *(21 sts)*

Row 4: Ch 1, sc dec in first 2 sts, sc in each of next 17 sts, sc dec in last 2 sts, turn. *(19 sts)*

Row 5: Ch 1, sc dec in first 2 sts, sc in each of next 15 sts, sc dec in last 2 sts, turn. *(17 sts)*

Row 6: Ch 1, sc dec in first 2 sts, sc in each of next 13 sts, sc dec in last 2 sts, turn. *(15 sts)*

Rows 7 & 8: Ch 1, sc each st across, turn. At end of last row, fasten off.

Edging

Rnd 1: Now working in rnds, join in any st at center back of Hat, ch 1, sc in each st around, working 1 sc in each row end on Visor and 3 sc in each corner, join in first st.

Rnd 2: Ch 1, sc in each st around, join in first st. Fasten off. ●

Dapper Diamonds

Skill Level
 INTERMEDIATE

Finished Sizes
Instructions given fit child's size small; changes for medium and large are in [ ].

Finished Measurements
Circumference: 19 *(small)* [23 *(medium)*, 26 *(large)*] inches

Height: 7½ *(small)* [8 *(medium)*, 8½ *(large)*] inches

Materials

- Premier Yarns Deborah Norville Alpaca Dance medium (worsted) weight acrylic/alpaca yarn (3½ oz/ 371 yds/100g per skein):
    1 skein each #0007 lemon lime and #0020 artichoke
- Size H/8/5mm crochet hook or size needed to obtain gauge
- Tapestry needle
- Stitch marker
- 6-inch-wide piece of cardboard

Gauge
Rnds 1 and 2 = 2 inches in diameter

Pattern Notes
Weave in ends as work progresses.

Work in continuous rounds; do not turn or join unless otherwise stated.

Mark first stitch of round. Mover marker as work progresses.

Join with slip stitch as indicated unless otherwise stated.

Hat
Rnd 1: With lemon lime, ch 2, 10 hdc in first ch, **do not join** *(see Pattern Notes)*, **place marker** *(see Pattern Notes)* in first st. *(10 sts)*

Rnd 2: 2 hdc in each st around. *(20 sts)*

Rnd 3: [Hdc in next st, 2 hdc in next st] around. *(30 sts)*

Rnd 4: [Hdc in each of next 2 sts, 2 hdc in next st] around. *(40 sts)*

Rnd 5: [Hdc in each of next 3 sts, 2 hdc in next st] around. *(50 sts)*

Rnd 6: [Hdc in each of next 4 sts, 2 hdc in next st] around. *(60 sts)*

Sizes Medium & Large Only
Rnd [7]: [Hdc in each of next 5 sts, 2 hdc in next st] around. *([70] sts)*

Size Large Only
Rnd [8]: [Hdc in each of next 6 sts, 2 hdc in next st] around. *([80] sts)*

All Sizes
Rnds 7–13 [8–14, 9–15]: Following Color Chart, hdc in each st around, working with both lemon lime and artichoke in each rnd, **changing color** *(see Stitch Guide)* as chart indicates and working over color not in use. At end of last rnd, fasten off artichoke.

Rnds 14–18 [15–19, 16–21]: Hdc in each st around.

Rnd 19 [20, 22]: Hdc in each st around, changing color to artichoke in last st. Fasten off lemon lime.

Rnd 20 [21, 23]: Hdc in each st around.

Rnd 21 [22, 24]: [Hdc in each of next 8 sts, **hdc dec** *(see Stitch Guide)* in next 2 sts] around. *(50 [60, 70] sts)*

Rnd 22 [23, 25]: Hdc in each st around, **join** *(see Pattern Notes)* in first st.

Fasten off.

Pompom
Make 1.

Wrap strand of artichoke around piece of cardboard 40 times or to desired thickness. Remove from cardboard and tie in center with 4-inch strand of same color. Cut lps and trim ends to desired shape. Use center strand to tie Pompom securely to top of Hat.

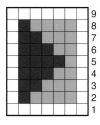

Dapper Diamonds
Color Chart

COLOR KEY	
⬜	Lemon lime
⬛	Artichoke

Fab Flap

Skill Level
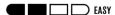 EASY

Finished Sizes
Instructions given fit child's size small; changes for medium and large are in [ ].

Finished Measurements
Circumference: 17 *(small)* [18½ *(medium)*, 20 *(large)*] inches

Height: 6½ *(small)* [7½ *(medium)*, 7¾ *(large)*] inches, excluding Earflaps

Materials
- Premier Yarns Deborah Norville Everyday Soft Worsted medium (worsted) weight acrylic yarn (4 oz/203 yds/113g per skein):
    1 skein each #1023 mist and #1018 cornflower
- Size G/6/4mm crochet hook or size needed to obtain gauge
- Tapestry needle
- Stitch markers
- ⅞-inch buttons: 2
- Sewing needle and matching thread

Gauge
Rnds 1–4 = 2 inches in diameter

Pattern Notes
Weave in ends as work progresses.

To change color, finish last stitch, drop old color, yarn over with new color and pull through st to join round.

Hat is worked in joined rounds with right side always facing; do not turn unless otherwise stated.

Join with slip stitch as indicated unless otherwise stated.

Mark first stitch of round. Move marker as work progresses.

Hat
Rnd 1 (RS): With mist, ch 2, 6 sc in first ch, **change color** *(see Pattern Notes)* to cornflower, **join** *(see Pattern Notes)* in first st, **place marker** *(see Pattern Notes)* in first st. *(6 sts)*

Rnd 2: Ch 1, 2 sc in each st around, change color to mist, join in first st. *(12 sts)*

Rnd 3: Ch 1, sc in first st, 2 sc in next st, *sc in next st, 2 sc in next st, rep from * around, change color to cornflower, join in first st. *(18 sts)*

Rnd 4: Ch 1, sc in first 2 sts, 2 sc in next st, *sc in each of next 2 sts, 2 sc in next st, rep from * around, change color to mist, join in first st. *(24 sts)*

Rnd 5: Ch 1, sc in first 3 sts, 2 sc in next st, *sc in each of next 3 sts, 2 sc in next st, rep from * around, change color to cornflower, join in first st. *(30 sts)*

Rnd 6: Ch 1, sc in each of first 4 sts, 2 sc in next st, *sc in each of next 4 sts, 2 sc in next st, rep from * around, change color to mist, join in first st. *(36 sts)*

Rnd 7: Ch 1, sc in each of first 5 sts, 2 sc in next st, *sc in each of next 5 sts, 2 sc in next st, rep from * around, change color to cornflower, join in first st. *(42 sts)*

Rnd 8: Ch 1, sc in each of first 6 sts, 2 sc in next st, *sc in each of next 6 sts, 2 sc in next st, rep from * around, change color to mist, join in first st. *(48 sts)*

Rnd 9: Ch 1, sc in each of first 7 sts, 2 sc in next st, *sc in each of next 7 sts, 2 sc in next st, rep from * around, change color to cornflower, join in first st. *(54 sts)*

Rnd 10: Ch 1, sc in each of first 8 sts, 2 sc in next st, *sc in each of next 8 sts, 2 sc in next st, rep from * around, change color to mist, join in first st. *(60 sts)*

Sizes Medium & Large Only
Rnd [11]: Ch 1, sc in each of first 9 sts, 2 sc in next st, *sc in each of next 9 sts, 2 sc in next st, rep from * around, change to cornflower, join in first st. *([66] sts)*

Size Medium Only
Rnd [12]: Ch 1, sc in each st around, change to mist, join in first st.

Size Large Only
Rnd [12]: Ch 1, sc in each of first 10 sts, 2 sc in next st, *sc in each of next 10 sts, 2 sc in next st, rep from * around, change to mist, join in first st. *([72] sts)*

All Sizes
Rnd 11 [13, 13]: Ch 1, sc in each st around, change color to cornflower, join in first st.

Rnd 12 [14, 14]: Ch 1, sc in each st around, change color to mist, join in first st.

Rnds 13–22 [15–26, 15–28]: [Rep last 2 rows alternately] 5 [6, 7] times. At end of last rnd, fasten off cornflower.

Rnd 23 [27, 29]: Ch 1, sc in each st around, do not join.

Rnds 24–27 [28–31, 30–33]: Sc in each st around.

Rnd 28 [32, 34]: Sc in each st around, join in first st. Fasten off.

Earflap

Getting started: Fold Hat in half and mark sts on each side of last rnd.

Row 1: Now working in rows, join mist in first marked st, ch 1, sc in same st and in each of next 8 sts, leaving rem sts unworked, turn. *(9 sc)*

Rows 2–6: Ch 1, sc in each st across, turn.

Row 7: Ch 1, **sc dec** *(see Stitch Guide)* in first 2 sts, sc in each of next 5 sts, sc dec in last 2 sts, turn. *(7 sts)*

Row 8: Ch 1, sc dec in first 2 sts, sc in each of next 3 sts, sc dec in last 2 sts, turn. *(5 sts)*

Row 9: Ch 1, sc dec in first 2 sts, sc in next st, sc dec in last 2 sts. Fasten off. *(3 sts)*

Rep at marker on opposite side of Hat for 2nd Earflap.

Edging

Rnd 1: Now working in rnds, join mist in first st on center back of Hat, ch 1, sc in each st around Hat, working 1 sc in each row end along sides of Earflaps, join in first st. Fasten off.

Hat Flap

Row 1: Now working in rows, join mist in first st on Hat after Earflap, working in **front lp** *(see Stitch Guide)*, sc in each st across to opposite Earflap, turn.

Rows 2–12: Ch 1, sc in each st across, turn. At end of last row, fasten off.

Finishing

Fold Hat Flap up on Hat. With sewing needle and thread and working through all thicknesses, sew one button on each corner of Hat Flap using photo as a guide. ●

Pink Perfection

Skill Level
 EASY

Finished Sizes
Instructions given fit child's size small; changes for medium and large are in [ ].

Finished Measurements
Hat circumference: 18 *(small)* [21 *(medium)*, 24 *(large)*] inches

Height: 7½ *(small)* [8 *(medium)*, 8½ *(large)*] inches

Flower: 3 inches in diameter

Materials
- Premier Yarns Ever Soft medium (worsted) weight acrylic yarn (3 oz/158 yds/85g per skein):
  1 skein each #0007 precious pink and #0010 raspberry
- Size F/5/3.75mm crochet hook or size needed to obtain gauge
- Tapestry needle
- Stitch marker

Gauge
Rnds 1–4 = 3½ inches in diameter

Pattern Notes
Weave in ends as work progresses.

Join with slip stitch as indicated unless otherwise stated.

Work in joined rounds with right side always facing; do not turn unless otherwise stated.

Mark first stitch of round. Move marker as work progresses.

Chain-2 at beginning of round does not count as a stitch unless otherwise stated.

Chain-4 at beginning of Flower counts as first double crochet and chain-1 space.

Hat

Rnd 1: With pink, ch 4, 10 dc in first ch, **join** (see Pattern Notes) in first st, **place marker** (see Pattern Notes) in first st. (10 dc)

Rnd 2: Ch 2 (see Pattern Notes), 2 dc in each st around, join in first st. (20 dc)

Rnd 3: Ch 2, dc in first st, 2 dc in next st, *dc in next st, 2 dc in next st, rep from * around, join in first st. (30 dc)

Rnd 4: Ch 2, dc in each of first 2 sts, 2 dc in next st, *dc in each of next 2 sts, 2 dc in next st, rep from * around, join in first st. (40 dc)

Rnd 5: Ch 2, dc in each of first 3 sts, 2 dc in next st, *dc in each of next 3 sts, 2 dc in next st, rep from * around, join in first st. (50 dc)

Rnd 6: Ch 2, dc in each of first 4 sts, 2 dc in next st, *dc in each of next 4 sts, 2 dc in next st, rep from * around, join in first st. (60 dc)

Sizes Medium & Large Only

Rnd [7]: Ch 2, dc in each of first 5 sts, 2 dc in next st, *dc in each of next 5 sts, 2 dc in next st, rep from * around, join in first st. ([70] dc)

Size Large Only

Rnd [8]: Ch 2, dc in each of first 6 sts, 2 dc in next st, *dc in each of next 6 sts, 2 dc in next st, rep from * around, join in first st. ([80] dc)

All Sizes

Rnd 7 [8, 9]: Ch 2, 3 dc in first st, sk next 2 sts, *3 dc in next st**, sk next 2 sts, rep from * around, ending last rep at **, sk next 2 [3, 1] sts, join in first st. (20 [23, 27] 3-dc groups)

Rnds 8–15 [9–16, 10–17]: 3 dc in each sp between 3-dc groups around, join in first st. At end of last rnd, fasten off pink.

Rnd 16 [17, 18]: Join raspberry in first st, ch 2, dc in each st around, join in first st. (60 [69, 81] dc)

Size Small Only

Rnds 17 & 18: Ch 2, dc in each st around, join in first st. At end of last rnd, fasten off raspberry.

Sizes Medium & Large Only

Rnd [18, 19]: Ch 2, dc in each of first [7, 9] dc, **dc dec** (see Stitch Guide) in next 2 sts, *dc in each of next 8 sts, dc dec in next 2 sts; rep from * around, join in first st. ([62, 73] sts)

Rnd [19, 20]: Ch 2, dc in each st around, join in first st. Fasten off raspberry.

All Sizes

Rnd 19 [20, 21]: Join pink in first st, ch 1, loosely sl st in each st around, join in first st. Fasten off.

Flower

Rnd 1: With pink, ch 4, join in first ch to form ring, **ch 4** (see Pattern Notes), [dc in ring, ch 1] 7 times, join in 3rd ch of beg ch-4. (8 dc, 8 ch-1 sps)

Rnd 2: (Sl st, ch 1, 3 dc, ch 1, sl st) in each ch-1 sp around, join in sp between first and last petal. Fasten off pink. (8 petals)

Rnd 3: Join raspberry in sp between 2 petals, ch 3, sl st in sp between next 2 petals, rep from * around. (8 ch-3 sps)

Rnd 4: (Sl st, ch 1, dc, 2 tr, dc, ch 1, sl st) in each ch-3 sp around, join in sp between first and last petal. Fasten off. (8 petals)

Finishing

Sew Flower on Hat as shown in photo or as desired. ●

Dancing Rainbow

Skill Level
 ■■□□ EASY

Finished Sizes
Instructions given fit child's size small; changes for medium and large are in [ ].

Finished Measurements
Circumference: 16 (small) [18 (medium), 19½ (large)] inches

Height: 6½ (small) [7 (medium), 8 (large)] inches

Flower: 3¼ inches in diameter

Materials
- Universal Yarn Uptown Worsted Tapestry medium (worsted) weight acrylic yarn (3½ oz/ 180 yds/100g per skein):
  - 1 skein #802 party time
- Size G/6/4mm crochet hook or size needed to obtain gauge
- Tapestry needle
- Stitch marker

Gauge
Rnds 1–7 = 4 inches in diameter

Pattern Notes
Weave in ends as work progresses.

Work in continuous rounds; do not turn or join unless otherwise stated.

Mark first stitch of round. Move marker as work progresses.

Join with slip stitch as indicated unless otherwise stated.

Chain-2 at beginning of round does not count as a stitch unless otherwise stated.

Hat
Rnd 1: Ch 2, 6 sc in first ch, **do not join** (see Pattern Notes), **place marker** (see Pattern Notes) in first st. (6 sts)

Rnd 2: 2 sc in each st around. (12 sts)

Rnd 3: [Sc in next st, 2 sc in next st] around. (18 sts)

Rnd 4: [Sc in each of next 2 sts, 2 sc in next st] around. (24 sts)

Rnd 5: [Sc in each of next 3 sts, 2 sc in next st] around. (30 sts)

Rnd 6: [Sc in each of next 4 sts, 2 sc in next st] around. (36 sts)

Rnd 7: [Sc in each of next 5 sts, 2 sc in next st] around. (42 sts)

Rnd 8: [Sc in each of next 6 sts, 2 sc in next st] around. (48 sts)

Rnd 9: [Sc in each of next 7 sts, 2 sc in next st] around. (54 sts)

Rnd 10: [Sc in each of next 8 sts, 2 sc in next st] around. (60 sts)

Sizes Medium & Large Only
Rnd [11]: [Sc in each of next 9 sts, 2 sc in next st] around. ([66] sts)

Size Large Only
Rnd [12]: [Sc in each of next 10 sts, 2 sc in next st] around. ([72] sts)

All Sizes

Rnds 11–27 [12–33, 13–39]: Sc in each st around.

Rnd 28 [34, 40]: Sc in each st around, **join** *(see Pattern Notes)* in first st.

Rnd 29 [35, 41]: Ch 2 *(see Pattern Notes)*, 2 dc in first sc, sk next 2 sc, *sl st in next sc, sk next 2 sc, 5 dc in next sc, sk next 2 sc, rep from * around to last 3 sc, sl st in next sc, sk next 2 sc, 3 dc in first sc, join in first dc. Fasten off. *(10 [11, 12] 5-dc groups)*

Flower

Back

Rnd 1: Ch 4, sl st in first ch to form ring, ch 1, 9 sc in ring, join in first st. *(9 sc)*

Rnd 2: (Ch 10, sl st, ch 10, sl st) in first st, *sl st in next st, (ch 10, sl st, ch 10, sl st) in same st, rep from * around. *(18 ch-10 lps)*

Fasten off.

Front

Rnd 1: Ch 4, sl st in first ch to form ring, ch 1, 6 sc in ring, join in first sc. *(6 sc)*

Rnd 2: (Ch 6, sl st, ch 6, sl st) in first st, *sl st in next st, (ch 6, sl st, ch 6, sl st) in same st, rep from * around. *(12 ch-6 lps)*

Fasten off.

Finishing

Position Front Flower on Back Flower. Working through all thicknesses, sew Flower on Hat around center, leaving petals loose as shown in photo. ●

Ripples & Roses

Skill Level

 EASY

Finished Sizes

Instructions given fit child's size small/medium; changes for medium/large are in [ ].

Finished Measurements

Circumference: 19 *(small/medium)* [21 *(medium/large)*] inches

Height: 7¼ *(small/medium)* [8¼ *(medium/large)*] inches

Small Rose: 1 inch in diameter

Large Rose: 1¾ inch in diameter

Materials

- Universal Yarn Deluxe Worsted Superwash medium (worsted) weight wool yarn (3½ oz/220 yds/100g per skein):
    - 1 skein each #731 burrow, #728 pulp and #723 petit pink
- Size F/5/3.75mm crochet hook or size needed to obtain gauge
- Tapestry needle
- Stitch marker

Gauge

Rnds 1–5 = 4 inches in diameter

Pattern Notes

Weave in ends as work progresses.

Hat is worked in joined rounds with right side always facing; do not turn unless otherwise stated.

Join with slip stitch as indicated unless otherwise stated.

Mark first stitch of round. Move marker as work progresses.

Chain-2 at beginning of round does not count as a stitch unless otherwise stated.

To change color, finish last stitch, drop old color, yarn over with new color and pull through st to join round.

Hat

Rnd 1 (RS): With burrow, ch 4, 12 dc in first ch, **join** *(see Pattern Notes)* in first st, **place marker** *(see Pattern Notes)* in first st. *(12 sts)*

Rnd 2: Ch 2 *(see Pattern Notes)*, 2 dc in each st around, join in first st. *(24 sts)*

Rnd 3: Ch 2, dc in first st, 2 dc in next st, *dc in next st, 2 dc in next st, rep from * around, join in first st. *(36 sts)*

Rnd 4: Ch 2, dc in each of first 2 sts, 2 dc in next st, *dc in each of next 2 sts, 2 dc in next st, rep from * around, join in first st. *(48 sts)*

Rnd 5: Ch 2, dc in each of first 3 sts, 2 dc in next st, *dc in each of next 3 sts, 2 dc in next st, rep from * around, join in first st. *(60 sts)*

Rnd 6: Ch 2, dc in each of first 4 sts, 2 dc in next st, *dc in each of next 4 sts, 2 dc in next st, rep from * around, join in first st. *(72 sts)*

Rnd 7: Ch 2, dc in each of first 5 sts, 2 dc in next st, *dc in each of next 5 sts, 2 dc in next st, rep from * around, join in first st. *(84 sts)*

Rnd 8: Join pulp in first st, **drop burrow** *(see Pattern Notes)*, ch 2, working in **back lps** *(see Stitch Guide)*, 2 dc in first st, dc in each of next 3 sts, [**dc dec** *(see Stitch Guide)* in next 2 sts] twice, dc in each of next 3 sts, *2 dc in next st, dc in each of next 3 sts, [dc dec in next 2 sts] twice, dc in each of next 3 sts, rep from * around to last st, 2 dc in last st, join in first st, drop pulp.

Rnd 9: With burrow, rep rnd 8.

Rnds 10–13 [10–15]: [Rep rnds 8 and 9 alternately] 2 [3] times. At end of last rnd, fasten off pulp.

Rnd 14 [16]: With burrow, ch 2, dc in each of first 5 sts, dc dec in next 2 sts, *dc in each of next 5 sts, dc dec in next 2 sts, rep from * around, join in first st. *(72 sts)*

Size Small/Medium Only

Rnd 15: Ch 2, dc in each of first 4 sts, dc dec in next 2 sts, *dc in each of next 4 sts, dc dec in next 2 sts, rep from * around, join in first st. *(60 sts)*

Both Sizes

Rnd 16 [17–20]: Ch 2, dc in each st around, join in first st. At end of last rnd, fasten off burrow. *(60 [72] sts)*

Rnd 17 [21]: Join pulp in first st, ch 1, sc in each st around, join in first st. Fasten off.

Small Rose
Make 2.

Row 1: With pink, ch 35, sc in 2nd ch from hook and in each rem ch across. Leaving long end for sewing, fasten off.

Beg at one end of row and sewing as work progresses, spiral foundation ch to form Rose.

Large Rose
Make 1.

Row 1: With pink, ch 60, sc in 2nd ch from hook and in each rem ch across. Leaving long end for sewing, fasten off.

Beg at one end of row and sewing as work progresses, spiral foundation ch to form Rose.

Finishing
Using photo as a guide, position Roses on Hat and sew in place. ●

Lizzy

Skill Level
 **EASY**

Finished Sizes
Instructions given fit child's size small; changes for medium and large are in [ ].

Finished Measurements
Circumference: 18 *(small)* [19½ *(medium)*, 21 *(large)*] inches

Height: 7 *(small)* [7¼ *(medium)*, 7¾ *(large)*] inches

Materials

- Berroco Comfort medium (worsted) weight acrylic/nylon yarn (3½ oz/210 yds/ 100g per skein):
  1 skein #9793 boysenberry heather
- Size G/6/4mm crochet hook or size needed to obtain gauge
- Tapestry needle
- Stitch marker

Gauge
Rnds 1–4 = 2 inches in diameter

Pattern Notes
Weave in ends as work progresses.

Work in continuous rounds; do not turn or join unless otherwise stated.

Mark first stitch of round. Move marker as work progresses.

Join with slip stitch as indicated unless otherwise stated.

Special Stitch
Shell: (2 dc, ch 1, 2 dc) in st or sp as indicated.

Hat
Rnd 1: Ch 2, 6 sc in first ch, **do not join** *(see Pattern Notes)*, **place marker** *(see Pattern Notes)* in first st. *(6 sts)*

Rnd 2: 2 sc in each st around. *(12 sts)*

Rnd 3: [Sc in next st, 2 sc in next st] around. *(18 sts)*

Rnd 4: [Sc in each of next 2 sts, 2 sc in next st] around. *(24 sts)*

Rnd 5: [Sc in each of next 3 sts, 2 sc in next st] around. *(30 sts)*

Rnd 6: [Sc in each of next 4 sts, 2 sc in next st] around. *(36 sts)*

Rnd 7: [Sc in each of next 5 sts, 2 sc in next st] around. *(42 sts)*

Rnd 8: [Sc in each of next 6 sts, 2 sc in next st] around. *(48 sts)*

Rnd 9: [Sc in each of next 7 sts, 2 sc in next st] around. *(54 sts)*

Rnd 10: [Sc in each of next 8 sts, 2 sc in next st] around. *(60 sts)*

Rnd 11: [Sc in each of next 9 sts, 2 sc in next st] around. *(66 sts)*

Sizes Medium & Large Only
Rnd [12]: [Sc in each of next 10 sts, 2 sc in next st] around. *([72] sts)*

Size Large Only
Rnd [13]: [Sc in each of next 11 sts, 2 sc in next st] around. *([78] sts)*

All Sizes
Rnd 12 [13, 14]: [Sk next 3 sts, **shell** *(see Special Stitch)* in next st] 16 [18, 19] times. *(16 [18, 19] shells)*

Rnds 13–19 [14–20, 15–22]: Shell in ch-1 sp of each shell around.

Rnd 20 [21, 23]: Ch 1, sc in each st around.

Rnds 21–23 [22–24, 24–26]: Sc in each st around.

Rnd 24 [25, 27]: Sc in each st around, **join** *(see Pattern Notes)* in first st. Fasten off. ●

Sweet Pea

Skill Level

 INTERMEDIATE

Finished Sizes

Instructions given fit child's size small; changes for medium and large are in [ ].

Finished Measurements

Circumference: 18 (small) [20 (medium), 22 (large)] inches

Height: 7 (small) [8 (medium), 9 (large)] inches

Flower: 4 inches in diameter

Materials

- Premier Yarns Deborah Norville Cotton Soft Silk medium (worsted) weight cotton/silk yarn (3 oz/154 yds/85g per skein):
  - 1 skein each #9505 aubergine and #9504 fuchsia flower
- Size G/6/4mm crochet hook or size needed to obtain gauge
- Tapestry needle
- Stitch marker

Gauge

Rnds 1–4 = 2 inches in diameter

Pattern Notes

Weave in ends as work progresses.

Work in continuous rounds; do not turn or join unless otherwise stated.

Mark first stitch of round. Move marker as work progresses.

Join with slip stitch as indicated unless otherwise stated.

Special Stitch

Surface stitch (surface st): Holding yarn at back of work, insert hook between rows, yo, pull lp through st and lp on hook.

Hat

Rnd 1: With aubergine, ch 2, 9 [10, 11] sc in first ch, **do not join** (see Pattern Notes), **place marker** (see Pattern Notes) in first st. (9 [10, 11] sts)

Rnd 2: 2 sc in each st around. (18 [20, 22] sts)

Rnd 3: [Sc in next st, 2 sc in next st] around. (27 [30, 33] sts)

Rnd 4: [Sc in each of next 2 sts, 2 sc in next st] around. (36 [40, 44] sts)

Rnd 5: [Sc in each of next 3 sts, 2 sc in next st] around. (45 [50, 55] sts)

Rnd 6: [Sc in each of next 4 sts, 2 sc in next st] around. (54 [60, 66] sts)

Rnd 7: [Sc in each of next 5 sts, 2 sc in next st] around. (63 [70, 77] sts)

Rnd 8: [Sc in each of next 6 sts, 2 sc in next st] around. (72 [80, 88] sts)

Rnds 9–31 [9–35, 9–39]: Sc in each st around. At end of last rnd, **join** (see Pattern Notes) in first st.

Lines

Join fuchsia, **surface st** (see Special Stitch) around rnd 16 [20, 24].

Rep on rnd 26 [30, 34].

Flower

Back

Rnd 1: With fuchsia, ch 4, sl st in first ch to form ring, ch 1, 8 sc in ring, join in first st. *(8 sc)*

Rnd 2: Ch 10, sl st in first st, *sl st in next st, ch 10, sl st in same st, rep from * around. *(8 ch-10 lps)*

Rnd 3: 12 sc in each ch-10 lp around, join in first sc. Fasten off.

Front

Rnd 1: With fuchsia, ch 4, sl st in first ch to form ring, ch 1, 6 sc in ring, join in first sc. *(6 sc)*

Rnd 2: Ch 6, sl st in first st, *sl st in next st, ch 6, sl st in same st, rep from * around. *(6 ch-6 lps)*

Rnd 3: 8 sc in each ch-6 lp around, join in first sc. Fasten off.

Finishing

Position Back Flower on Hat between Lines using photo as a guide. Sew each petal on Hat. Position Front Flower on Back Flower and sew in place around center, leaving petals loose. ●

STITCH GUIDE

STITCH ABBREVIATIONS

beg ....begin/begins/beginning
bpdc .... back post double crochet
bpsc ....back post single crochet
bptr ....back post treble crochet
CC.............................. contrasting color
ch(s) ....chain(s)
ch- .... refers to chain or space
    previously made (i.e., ch-1 space)
ch sp(s) ....chain space(s)
cl(s) ....cluster(s)
cm ....centimeter(s)
dc.....................double crochet (singular/plural)
dc dec........................ double crochet 2 or more
    stitches together, as indicated
dec........... decrease/decreases/decreasing
dtr .... double treble crochet
ext ....extended
fpdc ....front post double crochet
fpsc .... front post single crochet
fptr .... front post treble crochet
g.......................................gram(s)
hdc .... half double crochet
hdc dec...................half double crochet 2 or more
    stitches together, as indicated
inc .... increase/increases/increasing
lp(s) ....loop(s)
MC ....main color
mm ....millimeter(s)
oz.....................................ounce(s)
pc.....................................popcorn(s)
rem ....remain/remains/remaining
rep(s) ....repeat(s)
rnd(s) ....round(s)
RS ....right side
sc ....single crochet (singular/plural)
sc dec.....................single crochet 2 or more
    stitches together, as indicated
sk ....skip/skipped/skipping
sl st(s) .... slip stitch(es)
sp(s) .... space(s)/spaced
st(s) .... stitch(es)
tog..................................together
tr .... treble crochet
trtr ....triple treble
WS ....wrong side
yd(s) ....yard(s)
yo ....yarn over

YARN CONVERSION

OUNCES TO GRAMS	GRAMS TO OUNCES
1 .... 28.4	25 ....⅞
2 .... 56.7	40 .... 1⅔
3 .... 85.0	50 .... 1¾
4 .... 113.4	100 .... 3½

UNITED STATES		UNITED KINGDOM
sl st (slip stitch)	=	sc (single crochet)
sc (single crochet)	=	dc (double crochet)
hdc (half double crochet)	=	htr (half treble crochet)
dc (double crochet)	=	tr (treble crochet)
tr (treble crochet)	=	dtr (double treble crochet)
dtr (double treble crochet)	=	ttr (triple treble crochet)
skip	=	miss

Single crochet decrease (sc dec): (Insert hook, yo, draw lp through) in each of the sts indicated, yo, draw through all lps on hook.

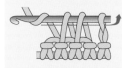

Example of 2-sc dec

Half double crochet decrease (hdc dec): (Yo, insert hook, yo, draw lp through) in each of the sts indicated, yo, draw through all lps on hook.

Example of 2-hdc dec

Reverse single crochet (reverse sc): Ch 1, sk first st, working from left to right, insert hook in next st from front to back, draw up lp on hook, yo and draw through both lps on hook.

Chain (ch): Yo, pull through lp on hook.

Single crochet (sc): Insert hook in st, yo, pull through st, yo, pull through both lps on hook.

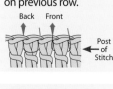

Double crochet (dc): Yo, insert hook in st, yo, pull through st, [yo, pull through 2 lps] twice.

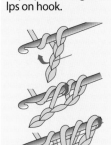

Double crochet decrease (dc dec): (Yo, insert hook, yo, draw lp through, yo, draw through 2 lps on hook) in each of the sts indicated, yo, draw through all lps on hook.

Example of 2-dc dec

Front loop (front lp) Back loop (back lp)

Front Loop Back Loop

Front post stitch (fp) Back post stitch (bp): When working post st, insert hook from right to left around post of st on previous row.

Back   Front

Post of Stitch

Half double crochet (hdc): Yo, insert hook in st, yo, pull through st, yo, pull through all 3 lps on hook.

Double treble crochet (dtr): Yo 3 times, insert hook in st, yo, pull through st, [yo, pull through 2 lps] 4 times.

Treble crochet decrease (tr dec): Holding back last lp of each st, tr in each of the sts indicated, yo, pull through all lps on hook.

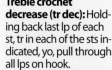

Example of 2-tr dec

Slip stitch (sl st): Insert hook in st, pull through both lps on hook.

Chain color change (ch color change) Yo with new color, draw through last lp on hook.

Double crochet color change (dc color change) Drop first color, yo with new color, draw through last 2 lps of st.

Treble crochet (tr): Yo twice, insert hook in st, yo, pull through st, [yo, pull through 2 lps] 3 times.

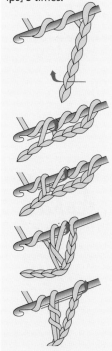

Metric Conversion Charts

METRIC CONVERSIONS

yards	x	.9144	=	metres (m)
yards	x	91.44	=	centimetres (cm)
inches	x	2.54	=	centimetres (cm)
inches	x	25.40	=	millimetres (mm)
inches	x	.0254	=	metres (m)

centimetres	x	.3937	=	inches
metres	x	1.0936	=	yards

INCHES INTO MILLIMETRES & CENTIMETRES (Rounded off slightly)

inches	mm	cm	inches	cm	inches	cm	inches	cm
1/8	3	0.3	5	12.5	21	53.5	38	96.5
1/4	6	0.6	5 1/2	14	22	56	39	99
3/8	10	1	6	15	23	58.5	40	101.5
1/2	13	1.3	7	18	24	61	41	104
5/8	15	1.5	8	20.5	25	63.5	42	106.5
3/4	20	2	9	23	26	66	43	109
7/8	22	2.2	10	25.5	27	68.5	44	112
1	25	2.5	11	28	28	71	45	114.5
1 1/4	32	3.2	12	30.5	29	73.5	46	117
1 1/2	38	3.8	13	33	30	76	47	119.5
1 3/4	45	4.5	14	35.5	31	79	48	122
2	50	5	15	38	32	81.5	49	124.5
2 1/2	65	6.5	16	40.5	33	84	50	127
3	75	7.5	17	43	34	86.5		
3 1/2	90	9	18	46	35	89		
4	100	10	19	48.5	36	91.5		
4 1/2	115	11.5	20	51	37	94		

KNITTING NEEDLES CONVERSION CHART

Canada/U.S.	0	1	2	3	4	5	6	7	8	9	10	10½	11	13	15
Metric (mm)	2	2¼	2¾	3¼	3½	3¾	4	4½	5	5½	6	6½	8	9	10

CROCHET HOOKS CONVERSION CHART

Canada/U.S.	1/B	2/C	3/D	4/E	5/F	6/G	8/H	9/I	10/J	10½/K	N
Metric (mm)	2.25	2.75	3.25	3.5	3.75	4.25	5	5.5	6	6.5	9.0

Annie's® *Happy Hats for Kids* is published by Annie's, 306 East Parr Road, Berne, IN 46711. Printed in USA. Copyright © 2015, 2016 Annie's. All rights reserved. This publication may not be reproduced in part or in whole without written permission from the publisher.

RETAIL STORES: If you would like to carry this publication or any other Annie's publication, visit AnniesWSL.com.

Every effort has been made to ensure that the instructions in this publication are complete and accurate. We cannot, however, take responsibility for human error, typographical mistakes or variations in individual work. Please visit AnniesCustomerService.com to check for pattern updates.

ISBN: 978-1-59012-276-1

2 3 4 5 6 7 8 9